AIKIDO

A beginner's guide

By Dunken Francis

WOODEN DRAGON PRESS

First published July 2003.

Cataloguing in Publication Data.

A Catalogue record for this book is available from the British Library.

ISBN 0-9545486-0-4

Printed by
Design & Print Centre Ltd.
www.DandPC.co.uk

Published by

WOODEN DRAGON PRESS

Orders & enquiries:
Email: aiki@DandPC.co.uk
Tel: +44 (0)1895 431373
Fax: +44 (0)1895 447683

Further details on The Institute of Aikido website
www.IOAikido.fsnet.co.uk

Dedicated to the memory of Sensei Tom Moss

Thank you to the following:

Sensei Foster, for guidance
Senseis Thackeray, Eder, Burlingham & Timms for their contributions
Sensei Davies, for letting me throw him around for days on end
Richard Max Goddard at Vivid Photography
and my wife, for her endless patience and support.

Contents

"Eight forces
sustain creation,
Movement & Stillness,
Solidification & Fluidity,
Extension & Contraction,
Unification & Division"

O'Sensei

Foreword

by Haydn W. Foster, 7th dan IA, Technical Director, Institute of Aikido

In this ever more sedentary world, where increasing numbers of us are earning a living by sitting all day in front of a computer, it is becoming more and more important to build some form of regular physical activity into our lives - and what better way than studying a beautiful martial art that not only looks after the physical, but nurtures the mental and spiritual into the bargain!

I began my Aiki career in the late 1950's, under the great Budo practitioner Kenshiro Abbe Sensei at The Hut Dojo in West London. 44 years later, I've seen Aikido in the United Kingdom grow from the original handful at The Hut, to the thousands of aikidoka now part of the great Aikido family in this country.

One often hears senior practitioners talking about "what they've done for Aikido". This is an attitude that always bemuses me. Over the years, I've not only had the privilege be part of the development in this country of what I believe to be one of the most complete and comprehensive martial arts in existence, but I've also had the opportunity to travel all over the world and meet some wonderful people.

"The Hut" Dojo, circa 1959, Kenshiro Abbe Sensei, centre

Would my life have been the same without Aiki? I don't think so.

When starting out on your Aikido "career" there will be hurdles to negotiate, but soon you will realise that Aikido is not just a system for self defence and well being, but a true budo "Way", in the sense that the lessons learnt on the tatami will stay with you and affect the way you live your life.

Initially it can be hard for new students to find the time for the two or three weekly practice sessions essential if one is to make progress, but once part of the weekly "schedule", Aikido quickly becomes integrated and part of one's daily life.

I wish to congratulate the author on the compiling of this beginner's guide and I'm sure it will be of great benefit to newcomers to our art.

Introduction

I'd like to make one point clear from the outset -
this book is in no way meant to be a technical manual!
There are already many superbly put together technical Aikido books
in existence, comprehensive in their descriptions and photographs,
covering all the varied styles and approaches to our beautiful art.

I remember only too clearly how daunting it was the first time I
stepped on the mat, faced with a seemingly endless stream of
information, and how hard it was for me to remember anything the
next day!

The first few months of practice can be very challenging, on many
levels and although there were times I started a class feeling quite
apprehensive or just "not in the mood" I can truthfully say I've never
ended a class in the same frame of mind.

The purpose of this book is to be a handy "aide memoire" for the
absolute newcomer to Aikido, in an attempt to help clarify the
potentially overwhelming series of movements, postures, attacks and
(for those not familiar with the Japanese language) the names and
phrases that make up our wonderful art.

I fully understand and accept that many of the techniques and
exercises shown here may be quite different to those practised within
the walls of your local dojo - That's fine - In my opinion, there are no
"styles" of Aikido, it's like a big pizza; you can cut it into slices or eat it
with a knife and fork, but it's still pizza!

The various sections within this book are present to
give a "snapshot" of Aikido, its structure, ethics and
heritage; hopefully this will whet your appetite enough
for you to go out and find out more for yourself, as you
travel on the Way.

Aikido

Aikido means "The Way of Harmony (of Spirit)". Morihei Ueshiba created a martial art he believed was capable of uniting the world - the principles of non-violence, conflict resolution and harmony at it's centre.

People of all ages, shapes and sizes can practice aikido as the techniques and movements in do not rely upon strength or force; the movements themselves encouraging increased flexibility and strength, as well as boosting self-confidence.

Traditionally, the system of Aikido is based around a series of key techniques, some of which finish in a throw, the others ending with the opponent being immobilised with a pin. All of these techniques can be practised from a set of formalised attacks. All of these techniques will in some way employ the key movements of Tai-sabaki (body turning), Tenkan (pivotal turning) and Irimi (entrance movement).

As a beginner, your early days should be spent learning "core skills" (posture, balance, basic body movement, ukemi, coordination, correct breathing etc), and many of the initial techniques that you will be shown will be from a wrist grab. It is not uncommon for newcomers to question the real-life application of such an attack. I am very thankful that early on in my aiki career I had this explained to me: The wrist grab techniques are your foundation, your basic technique.

Basic technique allows a beginner to start understanding how to correctly move an opponent who is holding on solidly, how to move out of the way of any follow-up attack, how to start developing your own "centre" and gives an overall feel for the techniques that you'll later be using against striking and other more advanced attacks. They also allow the beginner to "feel" what it's like to "receive" technique, and begin to understand the principles of safe falling.

If you can master a technique from a solid, static grasp, you can then apply this knowledge to moving techniques with a much more complete understanding of the movement.

Use of the wooden sword (bokken) and wooden staff (Jo) is common in many styles of aikido. The solo and pairs excercises in this aspect of the system should be regarded in a similar way to basic technique, in that they are not a system of learning to fight with weapons, but rather a tool to educate the body and mind in correct principles that will be needed to correctly perform body techniques.

In Aikido there are no "winners and losers". Aikido is an art of self-realisation, and, as your practice progresses, you will have to look inside yourself to find the resources necessary to meet the challenges aikido will present.

Dojo Etiquette

The dojo is a sacred place where we go to train physically, mentally and spiritually. Please take the following guidelines seriously, and be aware of any small differences in etiquette you may encounter when visiting other dojo's.

1   When entering or leaving the dojo, bow in the direction of O-Sensei's picture, the kamiza, or the front of the dojo. You should also bow when entering or leaving the mat.

2.   Never wear shoes on the mat - it is disrespectful and unhygienic. Always wear Zori (sandals) to and from the tatami. Zori should be left lined up neatly at the edge of the tatami.

3.   When the instructor comes onto the mat he/she and the students bow to O-Sensei's picture. The students then bow to the instructor formally to commence the training session.

4.   Many dojo's bow with senior grades nearer the Kamiza, or towards one end of the mat. If the dojo protocol does not include coloured belts, or you are not sure of where you should sit, sit at the back, or ask!

5.   Be on time for class. If you do happen to arrive late, sit quietly in seiza (kneeling) at the edge of the mat until the instructor invites you to join the practice.

6.   If you should have to leave the mat or dojo for any reason during class, always approach the instructor and ask permission. This is both out of respect to your teacher and for basic safety.

7.   Avoid sitting on the mat with your back to the picture of O-Sensei or the kamiza. Also, do not lean against the walls or sit with your legs stretched out (disrespectful and dangerous). Either sit in seiza or cross-legged, never slouched.

8.   Remove watches, rings and other jewellery before practice. Do not bring food or beverages into the dojo.

9.   Keep your finger and toe nails clean and cut short. Long nails are dangerous!

10.   Keep talking during class to a minimum. What conversation there is should be restricted to one topic - Aikido!

11.   Carry out instructions of the Sensei promptly.

12.   Do not engage in needless contests of strength or "wrestling matches" during class.

13.   Keep your training uniform clean, free from holes, tears and unpleasant odours.

14.   Pay your membership and mat fees promptly. The majority of clubs rely on this income to survive. If, for any reason, you are unable to pay your fees on time, talk with the person in charge. Reduced rates are sometimes available for students or those on low incomes.

15.   Never change your clothes (apart from hakama) on the mat.

16.   Remember that you are here to learn, and not to gratify your ego. Always train with an open mind.

17.   Preserve common-sense standards of decency and respect at all times.

18.   Before starting practice, visit the toilet (especially if you wear a hakama!) and remember to wash your hands.

19.   Try not to eat for an hour or so before each practice.

20.   Be aware of your own physical condition, stamina and physical strength. Don't try to do the impossible.

21.   The instructor should be referred to as Sensei ("Sen-say") during class and not by his/her first name.

22.   When the instructor claps, quickly sit down, listen and watch. When the instructor indicates to resume practice, bow to the instructor and continue practising. Change partners when the instructor indicates. When changing partners during class, one should acknowledge both your former partner and your new partner with a bow.

23.   When you are on the tatami, use the opportunity to clear your mind of all the "baggage" of daily life, leave your troubles behind, and fill your mind with Aikido!

Safe Stretching

Aikido, like any other physical activity, relies upon a healthy body.

A key factor in any physical regime is maintaining flexibility through proper stretching and although nearly all Aikido activity involves stretching in some form, it is still important to build correct stretching exercises into every pre-practice warm-up, and at the end of the session as part of the "warm-down".

Stretching is not the same as warming up! It is, however, a very important part of warming up. Warming up is quite literally the process of "warming up" or raising your core body temperature. A proper warm-up should raise your body temperature by one or two degrees Celsius. It is very important that you do your general warm-up **before** you stretch. Warming up can do more than just loosen stiff muscles; when done properly, it can actually improve muscle performance. On the other hand, a bad warm-up, or no warm-up at all, can increase your subsequent risk of injury.

Ideally, a particular stretch should work only the muscles you are trying to stretch. Isolating the muscles worked by a given stretch means that you do not have to worry about having to overcome the resistance offered by more than one group of muscles.

In general, the fewer muscles you try to stretch at once, the better.

Proper breathing is important when stretching. Correct breathing helps to relax the body, increases blood flow, and helps to remove lactic acid from muscles. Take slow, relaxed breaths when you stretch, exhaling as the muscle is stretched.

The proper way to breathe is to inhale slowly through the nose, expanding the abdomen (not the chest); hold the breath a moment; then exhale slowly through the nose or mouth.

Any decent Aikido instructor (especially those with Coaching qualifications) should know the difference between safe and unsafe stretches.

Basic rules of Stretching
• Warm up first
• Do not ballistic stretch ie. using a "bouncing" motion
• Don't hold your breath whilst stretching
• Stretch slowly and gently
• Try to hold your stretch for around 20-30 seconds
• Pain is your brain's way of telling you to stop!
• If it stretches tendons or ligaments, don't do it!

Tai no henko

O'Sensei always started his practices with tai-no-henko, and once said that a student could learn all the basics of Aikido if he practised just three techniques:

• Tai no henko
• Morotedori-kokyuho
• Suwariwaza-kokyuho

The tai no henko exercise contains within it many core principles of Aikido, and therefore should be practised as part of every training session.

By careful practice of tai no henko we are studying the principles of:

• Moving "off the line"
• Correct posture
• The "blending" & "extension" of Ki
• Maintaining connection with our partner
• Weight underside
• Breath-body coordination
• Tenkan (pivotal) movement

The key shapes of Aikido techniques & exercises

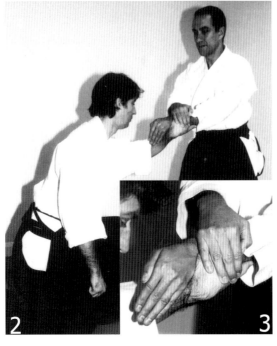

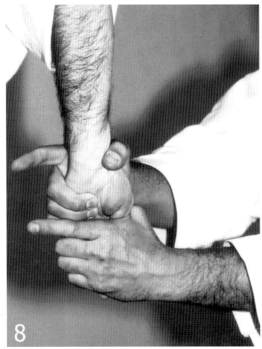

Key

1. Ikkyo ("1st Principle")
2. Ai-hamni Katatedori Nikkyo ("2nd principle")
3. Ai-hamni Katatedori Nikkyo detail
4. Nikkyo
5. Nikkyo application
6. Nikkyo application (variation)
7. Sankyo ("Third principle")
8. Sankyo detail
9. Sankyo application

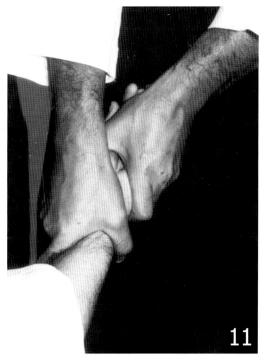

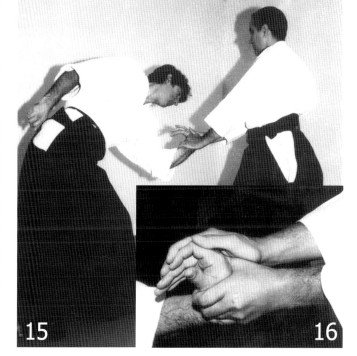

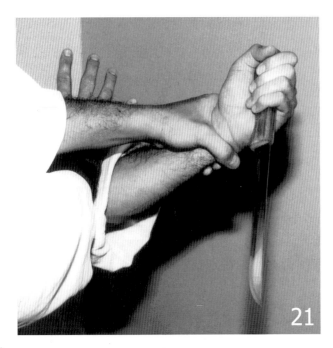

Key

24. Juji-garami/nage ("Crossed/entanglement arm" throw)

25. Sumi-otoshi ("Corner" throw)

26. Morotedori kokyu-ho (entrance)

27. Morotedori kokyu-ho (throw)

28. Aiki otoshi ("Aiki drop" throw) entrance

29. Aiki otoshi (throw)

Key

30. Nikkyo wrist exercise

31. Nikkyo wrist exercise (variation)

32. Kote-gaeshi wrist exercise

33. Wrist stretch exercise

34. Sankyo wrist exercise

35. Shikko (knee walking)

Aikido "Attacks"

Attacks should always be practised from both right and left sides but for convenience are described and shown from right stance only

*(1st Form)***Ai hanmi katatedori**
(Right) hand takes right wrist

*(2nd Form)***Gyaku hanmi katatedori**
(Right) hand takes left wrist

*(3rd Form)***Katadori**
(Right) hand takes left shoulder

*(4th Form)***Munedori**
(Right) hand takes lapel

*(5th Form)***Shomen uchi**
(Right) hand strikes centre of the head

*(6th Form)***Yokomen uchi**
(Right) hand strikes to the temple

(7th form) **Mune tsuki**
(Right) hand straight punch to adbomen

*(8th Form)***Ushiro eridori**
(Right) hand takes collar from behind

13

*(9th Form)***Hijidori**
(Right) hand takes left elbow

*(10th Form)***Morotedori** *Two hands*
(push around to) grab one wrist

*(11th Form)***Ryotedori** *Two hands*
grabbing both wrists from front

*(12th Form)***Ryokatadori**
Grabbing both shoulders from front

*(13th Form)***Ushiro ryotedori**
Both wrist grab, from behind

*(14th Form)***Ushiro ryohijidori**
Both elbows grab, from behind

*(15th Form)***Ushiro ryokatadori**
Both shoulders grab, from behind

*(16th Form)***Ushiro kubishime**
(Right) arm chokes, left hand
grabs left wrist, from behind

Aikido Attacks - variations

- *(3rd Form variation)*
  Kata dori men uchi
  (Right) hand takes right
  shoulder, left hand strikes head

- *(7th Form variation)*
  Jodan tsuki
  Straight punch to the face

- *(7th Form variation)*
  Chudan tsuki
  Straight punch to the solar
  plexus

- *(7th Form variation)*
  Gedan tsuki
  Straight punch to the
  groin/knee

Tegatana ("hand-blade" or "sword hand")

The tegatana is a specific hand shape used in Aikido to lead, control and/or make atemi. The name "hand-blade" or "sword hand" reflects the derivation of basic Aikido techniques from sword movements. Many Aikido movements extend and align "through" the initial movement of tegatana.

Seiza (sitting position)

Seiza is one of the most commonly used sitting postures in Japanese martial arts, with students assuming this posture at the beginning and end of practise sessions for formal bow, meditation etc. Aikido, in particular, makes use of seiza to teach basic movements, with technique being performed "on the knees" (Suwari-waza) and many Iai schools use seiza as a basis for basic forms.

The word seiza is written with two Chinese characters; "sei" meaning "correct, proper, true" (and by itself can be pronounced tadashii, meaning "just right" or "appropriate") and "za" meaning "sitting posture" (written with an ideograph that looks like people sitting on a raised floor under a roof).

In Japanese culture, sitting in seiza (kneeling, sitting on one's ankles) is the most correct, beautiful, and "proper" formal sitting posture, especially when seated indoors (usually on tatami matting).

Many people complain that seiza makes their feet "go to sleep" (known in Japan as "shibireru") but this tends to be from lack of proper exercise, weak leg muscles and poor circulation; not necessarily due to the position of sitting in seiza. If one is sitting correctly, one should be able to perform seiza for anything up to an hour a day without discomfort.

Proper seiza, helps to naturally align your body and spinal column, focusses on your "centre" and leads to an alert mind and body - hence its common use in meditation.

Different schools of martial arts may have slightly different versions of seiza, but for a rough guideline, sit in seiza as follows:

- Sit kneeling with your legs folded under you, with the left big toe on top of the other.
- The knees are about one to two fists apart .
- Sit with back up straight, but in a relaxed posture.
- Rest your hands naturally in your lap.

Counting in Japanese

Ichi	"Each"	ONE
Ni	"Nee"	TWO
San	"San"	THREE
Shi	"Shee"	FOUR
Go	"Go"	FIVE
Roku	"Rokku"	SIX
Shichi	"She-chee"	SEVEN
Hachi	"Hach"	EIGHT
Ku	"Kyu"	NINE
Ju	"Jyu"	TEN

Suwari Waza ("sitting technique")

Suwari Waza, or "sitting technique" covers a broad range of movements performed from a kneeling position.

Most of the basic Aikido techniques can be performed from a kneeling position and are an important aspect of the system as they promote correct use of the hips and encourage the principles of stability, balance and weight-underside.

Kokyu Doza
A fundamental exercise that can be performed in a number of ways, depending on your partner's grasp (i.e. whether uke is pushing down, is holding with stiff arms, is pushing forwards, pulling etc).

Kneeling about one fist apart, uke grasps both nage's wrists in the way of ryote dori, and tries to remain connected to nage throughout.

If the grip is weak or breaks off, connection is lost and there is little benefit to either party.

The key to this exercise is to try not to use strength, instead using extension of ki and tegatana try to unsettle uke's centre, and therefore his balance, whilst keeping your own centre stable.

In one variation, once uke has been unbalanced and taken to the ground, he should try to sit up again, with nage using only the principles of ki and weight-underside as restraint.

Hanmi handachi
Some techniques (Shiho-nage is a common example) can be performed "hanmi handachi" with the uke, or attacker standing and nage kneeling, many of these being derived from Samurai seated sword-drawing movements (originally developed to counter attacks whilst sitting or eating).

Basic (Kihon) Technique

Basic technique is the foundation of Aikido - if your basic technique is not correct, you will be unable to perform other techniques.

It is foolish to think that Aikido can be learnt by only practising fast, flowing gentle movements - this only encourages technical inaccuracy and martial inefficiency. As the old saying goes "You have to walk before you can run".

To attain technical excellence it is best to practice a high number of repetitions of slow, accurate basic technique, only then will you be able to perform flowing technique effectively.

Paradoxically, to become fast (and precise) we need to train slowly.

By the in-depth study of basic (kihon) technique, the practitioner of Aikido can one day get to the stage where body movement, technique and self defence become as one - an instinctive reaction to any situation.

"The strength of any martial art is in its basic technique"

"*Aikido can be likened to a massive tree full of branches and deep with foliage; the higher the tree gets, the thicker the base and the deeper the roots. Thus the analogy applies to our martial art inasmuch that if you want to understand truly the full extent of what the art has to offer then more attention is needed to honing your skills in basic technique. Without a broad base you will be limited as to how far you can grow. As it stands our system of basic solid, basic flowing and then full flowing technique represents a syllabus almost un-parallelled by any other martial art, which allows us the ability to "refer back" to see how a technique works in order to adapt this to the higher levels of Aikido where technique becomes less important, and pure body movement takes over. You must be able to walk before you can run, and so it follows then that the first months and/or even years of study are spent familiarising oneself with the basic in a solid format or with some movement. Once a technique is performed in "full flow", then it is fairly easy to throw your opponent as they seem to do most of the work for you, but should this same opponent take hold and become immoveable, then without the vital skills gained by continual study of basic technique, difficulties will be experienced".*

William Timms, 4th dan IA

Ukemi

Ukemi is the generic term used in Aikido for any movement uke has to do in response to nage's throw or pin, usually on their way to the floor! Ukemi is always thought of as a roll or fall, but the literal translation "receiving (through) the body" gives us a valuable insight into the true nature of this important aspect of Aikido, which many regard as an art in itself.

The principles of Aikido or "The Way of Harmony" are demonstrated clearly in properly executed ukemi. Ukemi begins at the moment when uke's attack, once received by nage, is then redirected. At this moment, uke must pro-actively harmonize with this redirection and follow the movement completely, otherwise he'll be thrown around (and land) like a sack of potatoes! By the same token, it is futile to try and "pre-empt" a throw as nage will simply change direction, making the resultant ukemi even more difficult to follow! To allow both nage and uke to truly benefit from the interaction, uke must be responsive. To "resist" a technique (at high level practice weak techniques can be responded to with kaeshiwaza but to resist is simply asking nage for an atemi!) or to simply "let yourself be thrown" without any attempt to follow the direction in which the techniques is being applied is not only an ineffective way to practise, but is downright dangerous!

Many of the (thankfully very few) serious accidents that have ever occurred in aikido have been where inexperienced students have been thrown and the combined lack of protection from nage and poor ukemi have resulted in injuries. Learning to fall correctly and safely is a wonderful skill to possess, but is so often left "un-taught" or it is assumed that the student will "teach themselves".

It is essential, from the very first time you step on the mat, that you study ukemi correctly. Always ukemi with correct "output", so that even on a basic "un-assisted" roll across the mat your shape will not "collapse", whilst at the same time making sure that you breathe out to encourage a good flow of ki - this will also help you to relax.

So, in conclusion, the basic aspects of ukemi to consider are:

• Always follow your partner, and blend with the movement.
• Always be pro-active - don't just "be thrown" (but don't "jump the gun" either).
• Respect your partner's ability - you may have to react quicker to a senior practitioner!
• Always put enough energy into your ukemi so that you can escape safely and hold your shape; a lazy ukemi is a dangerous ukemi.
• Don't hold your breath - coordinate your breathing with your movement.

Atemi

O'Sensei is often quoted as saying "Aikido is 70% atemi" (I've even heard 90% quoted!!). The word "Atemi" literally means "strike".

Atemi was developed in Asia thousands of years ago and was a martial art in itself, ironically aiming strikes at many of the points also used for healing in acupuncture and acupressure. The principles of Atemi eventually began to be assimilated into Japanese martial arts (Samurai especially began integrating atemi into their unarmed combat techniques).

In Aikido, the atemi is used in the following ways:

- To stop or re-direct your partner's intention, ki or movement.
- To "fill the gaps" or potential weaknesses during the application of technique.
- As a destructive force, if one is left with no ethical alternative.

To "take the mind"
An attack will be produced by an aggressive intention. One of the key roles of Atemi within aikido is to diffuse the attacker's intention, either by an applied counter strike or by simply leaving a disruptive force (fist/hand/tegatana/knee/foot etc) directly in the path of where a (vulnerable) part of your opponent will be, once they have committed to their attack.

For example, if your partner strikes with a straight punch to the face (Jodan tsuki), by moving off the line of attack Atemi can applied either as a strike, or can be positioned in such a way that your opponent's impetus lead him to "walk into" your Atemi.

In either instance, Atemi will serve both to disrupt the attacker's output of ki, and should make the physical aspect of the attack falter, even stop, allowing technique to be applied in a much more controlled manner (and therefore with more ethical choice) than if attempted against a "full speed" attack.

To "fill the gaps"
The other aspect of Atemi often neglected appears "within" technique. In an ideal situation, under perfect conditions, technique can be applied without Atemi, but in the real world this is unlikely, so Atemi is made to both "protect" the nage whilst carrying out technique and to further breakdown the attacker's resistance.

For example, when applying a technique like Gyakyu-hamni Kaiten-nage (a spiral throw which requires nage to enter under the attacker's arm), without correctly placed Atemi nage is left vulnerable to counter strikes; in this way we can see that the atemi is actually an integral part of the technique, not an afterthought.

Some styles of Aikido do not practise using Atemi, other styles use them comprehensively: whatever your practice protocol requires it is essential to always remember *where* the Atemi would occur within each technique you study, as in a real encounter you may need it!

The "last resort"
This brings us to the final aspect of Atemi - If all else fails, and it is appropriate in the situation, Atemi can be used as a destructive, even fatal strike. Advanced aikidoka will be aware of the many nerve points and areas of vulnerability which when struck with accurate Atemi can cause severe injury, even death (there are martial arts specifically concerned with Atemi to these "vital points"). This is a **last resort**, and when in a life-threatening situation, you use whatever you have available.

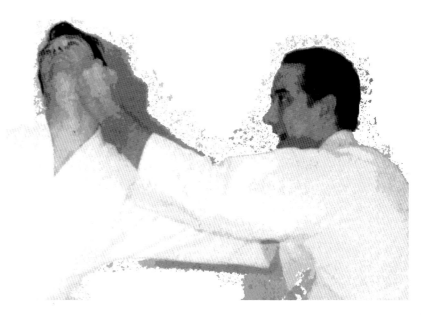

Ki

The concept of Ki has almost infinite interpretations - this concept of the fundamental life force is at the core of all "internal" martial arts, and its nature is ethereal and elusive - and often only realised through personal experience.

Koichi Tohei, senior student of Morihei Ueshiba and the founder of Ki no Kenkyukai explained ki as follows:

"Ki is the basic unit of the universe. It is the infinite gathering of infinitely small particles. Everything is ultimately composed of Ki. If you pursue this concept to the depth of human consciousness, you will understand the universal mind which governs all creation, loving and protecting all life... everything originates from the Ki of the universe"

Tohei sensei clearly perceived Ki to be the core substance of the entire universe. The importance he attached to Ki and its development is evident when practising Aikido with students of his organization, but from the above quotation we can see that he believed Ki was more than just energy to be manipulated for use in the martial arts.

In China, Ki is referred to as "Chi" or "Qi". Dr. Yang, Jwing-Ming, the founder of the YOAA, Inc. (an international organization dedicated to the preservation and practice of Chi-based arts) refers to Ki thus:

"Qi (Chi) is the foundation of all Chinese medical theory... It corresponds to the Greek "pnuema" and the Sanskrit "prana", it is considered to be the vital force and energy flow in all living things... Qi can be best explained as a type of energy very much like electricity, which flows through the human or animal body. When this circulation becomes stagnant or stops, the person or animal will become ill or die. Although there is no precise Western definition of Qi, it is often referred to as bioelectricity. In fact, it was recognized in the last decade that Qi is actually the bioelectricity circulating in all living things".

From the above quotes, it's easy to see that both the Chinese and Japanese views on this matter really don't differ all that much. Both "Ki masters" maintain that this biological energy is the basis of all life, and that without Ki/Chi/Qi, death certainly is the result. Neither of these eminent gentlemen imply that Ki can give one supernatural powers (as seen in so many martial arts cartoons) but both agree that "development" of our use of this universal force is indeed possible, and benefits the individual on a fundamental level.

Ki "exercises"
There are many exercises or "tests" in existence. These are used to demonstrate how well the body and spirit, or Ki are unified, by comparing the results obtained when performing these exercises with physical strength only and then again using the principles of ki.

The Unbreakable Circle

Make a circle with thumb and index finger - then get someone to force your fingers apart, using both thumbs and forefingers. If you simply tense your fingers, you'll see that your partner will easily force your fingers apart, but if you concentrate on the idea of the circle being unbroken, and keep relaxed, your fingers will not easily be parted.

The Unbendable Arm

There are several ways to perform this test. In this version, place your naturally extended arm on your partner's shoulder, palm turned inwards. Your partner should then attempt to bend your arm by exerting gradual but firm pressure. If you use only strength (and you are fairly evenly matched, strength-wise), your arm will eventually bend. If you visualise your ki flowing through your arm and out of the fingertips, and maintain relaxation, the arm should be much harder to bend.

This exercise is particularly useful for the beginner, as it demonstrates an important principle used not only in ukemi, but in many techniques.

The Unliftable Body

This is really more an exercise in the "weight underside" principle than a Ki test, however it is again useful for the beginner as it allows personal experience of a fundamental principle of Aikido. Get your partner to try to lift you by holding under the arms. First of all, try to "make yourself light" by breathing into your upper chest area and visualising all your weight spiralling upwards - then let him try again, this time relaxing and letting your centre drop to your lower abdomen. With practice, your partner will find moving you very difficult indeed!

The Riai system

The term, "Riai" literally means "a blending of truths". Riai teaches that tai-jutsu techniques were developed from movements using the sword. Therefore, it's sensible to assume that training using sword movements will develop tai-jutsu technique.

Riai involves a combined approach to training in three martial art systems; tai-jutsu, aiki-ken, and aiki-jo, each of which share a core of basic principles in body movement, application and philosophy. Aiki-ken and Aiki-jo were developed to complement tai-jutsu and create a complete martial art.

O-Sensei emphasized that a weapon should be used as an extension of the body, but also stressed that one should not develop a dependence upon a particular weapon. To build this feeling, one should study the basic exercises of ken and jo suburi, and the basic tai-jutsu techniques tai-no-henko and kokyu dosa. A good understanding of these basic exercises is essential for the development of correct tai-jutsu.

One of the key differences between Aikido and other martial arts is in the posture. When uke receives an attack, he must be standing in triangular posture. When standing in hito-e-mi (triangular posture), it is possible to make atemi (strike) without receiving a blow in return. Secondly, uke must blend with the ki of his attacker. The combination of these two principles contributes greatly to Aikido's uniqueness.

The second concept, the blending of ki, has many possibilities. In practice, one tries always to blend one's ki with that of the attacker. This allows one to respond in a controlled manner, without striking, even when it is possible to do so. Partner blending weapons practices such as awase are done from basic forms as their purpose is the development of the harmony of ki.

*"To understand the combined riai Aikido system is to realise that one is not dependent upon a ken, jo or other weapon. When using a Bokken or Jo, don't think of them as "weapons" in their own right, but **feel the relationship to your body movement in taijutsu.**" Saito Sensei*

It should be the aim of all who practise Aikido to develop ki, body, and mind through daily practice. In this way, one can develop the true spirit of Aikido.

Practising Suburi

It is important to do all suburi with full focus and extension of ki. One suburi done with full intent and flow of ki is much better than thousands done without commitment or focus.

All suburi are performed from triangular posture. The handle of the ken is held roughly over the centre/two inches below the navel. This alignment makes movement forward and backward and right and left easier.

In the first suburi, it is important that the sword be raised overhead and cut down in a vertical line through the body. As in all Aikido suburi, during the downward stroke of the sword, the hips must be solidly based. The cut "unfurls" from the shoulders, through the elbows to the wrists.

The bokken cut is initiated from the little finger with full connection between the palm of the hand and wood. The grip tightens in the direction of the thumbs at the end of each cut. A similar grip is used in taijutsu.

Mental Attitude of Weapons Partner Practice:

In Aikido weapons practice with a partner the most important thing is to "catch the ki" and harmonize with your opponent.

Practice with the Bokken (wooden sword)

All the points mentioned in the "practise with the Jo" section apply here - careful practise of Aiki-ken suburi and awase will not make you a great swordsman but are invaluable in the development of correct tai-jutsu principles.

As with the use of the Jo, Aiki-ken movements are virtually all based upon the basic suburi. There are seven ken suburi and these are described below:

First Suburi
Basic shomen (straight) cut. From "Ken kamae" or basic "sword stance", raise the sword so that your left hand is above your forehead and the bokken is angled slightly back. Bring your front (right) foot back slightly as you raise the bokken. During this movement your hips should turn from a triangular orientation to a square one. Cut down (remember "shoulders, elbows, wrists") with a wringing motion, as if you were flinging something off the tip of the bokken, and let your hips return to their triangular position. Finish with the bokken in front of your centre. Always cut to end horizontal to the floor. At all times keep the bokken within the plane of your centerline. Always cut with relaxed shoulders.

Second Suburi
From the ready position, step back deeply with the right foot and raise the sword so that the left hand is just above the forehead. Ensure that the left hip is turned forwards). Step forward, drop in the right hip and perform a shomen cut.

Third Suburi ("Sword of Universal Ki")
Start the same as number 2, except the sword raise pauses very briefly above the head whilst the intake of breath "draws in Ki" (it is useful to visualise the energy flowing down into the bokken from above in a great spiral), then the breath is dropped down to the centre as the sword is "layed down" so that it is almost resting on the right hip ("waki kamae"). Step forward with the right foot, drop the right hip and perform a shomen cut, making sure the sword comes directly down the centre line, with plenty of Ki-ai!!

Fourth Suburi
Start as 2nd suburi, stepping forwards on the right foot to perform a shomen cut. Now step forward with the left foot and perform a shomen cut. During each "step", ensure the hips are engaged. Continue this process while alternating feet. May be performed walking forwards or on the spot with alternating feet.

Fifth Suburi
Start as 2nd suburi, stepping forwards on the right foot to perform a shomen cut.

As the left foot starts to step forward, drop the tip of the bokken down to the right whilst lifting the hilt up to the forehead.

Continue bringing the tip of the bokken around to behind the head, then cut down through the centre. Now drop the tip of the bokken down to the left side, and repeat as before, stepping forwards on the right foot. At the end of each "step", ensure the hips are engaged. Alternate left and right in this way. May be performed walking forwards or on the spot with alternating feet.

Sixth Suburi
This suburi is the same as number 5, with one addition; in between each cut slide forward slightly and perform a "tsuki" on that side. The tsuki is a thrust to the mid-section with the tip of the bokken. Slide forward slightly with the front foot and turn the blade so that it faces the opposite side from the front foot, e.g., a right tsuki has the right foot forward and the blade facing left. Again, alternate left and right in this way, whilst advancing forwards.

Seventh Suburi
As sixth suburi, but this time the tsuki movement is performed on the opposite side to the cut - ie cut on the right foot, tsuki on the left foot etc. Repeat, whilst advancing forwards.

"Cutting through the centre"

Waki kamae

Practice with the Jo (wooden Staff)

As discussed in the "Riai" section - the careful study of both the Bokken and Jo is invaluable in developing the correct posture and body movement principles that are fundamental to efficient tai-jutsu (body technique). There are many varied jo kata in existence but nearly all are made up of movements from the basic 20 suburi, which can in turn be broken into thrusting, striking, wrist, hasso and flowing/turning groups. "Hasso" translated means "figure-eight" stance, but doesn't refer to the arabic/western figure 8 but to the Japanese character for eight (a shape resembling the roof of a house - the hasso position with the sword or jo held upright to the side of the head and the elbows slanting down making the same shape).

The "Thrust" group (Tsuki no bu)

1st suburi	choku - tsuki
2nd suburi	kaeshi - tsuki
3rd suburi	ushiro - tsuki
4th suburi	tsuki gedan - gaeshi
5th suburi	tsuki jodan - gaeshi

The "Strike" group (Shomen no bu)

6th suburi	shomen uchikomi
7th suburi	renzoku uchikomi
8th suburi	(sho) men - uchi gedan - gaeshi
9th suburi	(sho) men - uchi ushiro - tsuki
10th suburi	gyaku-yokomen (uchi) ushiro - tsuki

The "Wrist" group (katate no bu)

11th suburi	katate gedan gaeshi
12th suburi	katate toma - uchi
13th suburi	katate hachi - no - ji - gaeshi

The "Hasso" group (Hasso no bu)

14th suburi	hasso - gaeshi - uchi
15th suburi	hasso - gaeshi - tsuki
16th suburi	hasso - gaeshi ushiro - tsuki
17th suburi	hasso - gaeshi ushiro - uchi
18th suburi	hasso - gaeshi ushiro - harai (pronounced "barai")

The "Flowing turn" group (Nagare gaeshi no bu)

19th suburi	hidari nagare - gaeshi - uchi
20th suburi	migi nagare - gaeshi - tsuki
"21st suburi"	(19 & 20 sometimes merged together to form 21)

Basic principles of Aiki-jo

- Always cut "through your centre" - never "over the shoulder".
- Maintain correct posture at all times.
- Finish all cuts horizontally/parallel to the floor.
- Ensure that all cuts are made with the hip engaged, ie. drop the front hip to make sure the cut is performed with power from the hips and centre, and not just from the arms and wrists.
- Grip "with ki" - in a relaxed but controlled manner, with the main connection being made with the little, ring and middle fingers, and the index finger relaxed.
- When practising with a partner, the most important issue is to "blend" or coordinate with their movements.

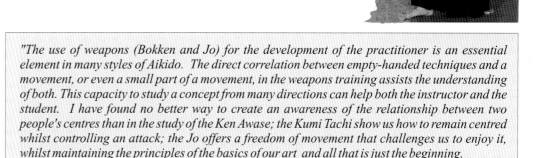

"The use of weapons (Bokken and Jo) for the development of the practitioner is an essential element in many styles of Aikido. The direct correlation between empty-handed techniques and a movement, or even a small part of a movement, in the weapons training assists the understanding of both. This capacity to study a concept from many directions can help both the instructor and the student. I have found no better way to create an awareness of the relationship between two people's centres than in the study of the Ken Awase; the Kumi Tachi show us how to remain centred whilst controlling an attack; the Jo offers a freedom of movement that challenges us to enjoy it, whilst maintaining the principles of the basics of our art and all that is just the beginning.

Training with weapons develops and forges the practitioner's body, mind and spirit in such a direct way that it can almost be seen as a 'shortcut' compared with concentrating solely on empty-handed technique. Any student who studies the system of empty-handed technique, Bokken and Jo, and their interrelationship will be working with a tradition which will delight them with the many insights it offers year on year."

Simon Thackeray, 4th dan IA

Seminars

Whether you've been training 1 week or 10 years, you'll always learn something new at a seminar. If you're really nervous about training at a different dojo with a different style just go along and watch (although nothing beats actually participating). Watching seminars and classes is another form of training known as "mitori geiko".

Firstly, always mark your name clearly on all your equipment - your dogi, bokken, jo, hakama and especially your zori - I've lost several pairs in the rush to get to the half-time refreshments!

If the seminar is more than a few sessions, make sure you bring more than one dogi. You'll be much more comfortable in later sessions if you have a fresh, dry kit to wear.

If you are travelling by plane and will be taking weapons (bokken, jo, shinai, tanto) with you, never use the term "weapons" when you check in your luggage. Airport security is rightly very strict now, and people have been detained by the authorities who were unaware what a bokken was. Never, ever take a tanto on board in your hand luggage - you will be arrested. When checking in your weapons bag, use descriptive terms like "training sticks" or "exercise sticks" to avoid problems.

Drink plenty of water (not tea or coffee, these are diuretics and make you dehydrate) at least an hour before training - dehydration causes loss of both mental and physical performance. Asking to leave the mat during a practice for a drink of water is considered bad etiquette in most dojo's.

Make sure you have eaten - again, at least an hour before training, and preferably something easily digestible; fruit is ideal. Another good idea is to have a decent meal of carbohydrates (potatoes, rice, pasta etc) the night before, as this will release energy during the following day.

Whenever possible, follow the "when in Rome..." rule. There is no point in going to a seminar to see other people's aiki, only to then get up and practise exactly how you do "normally". Watch what the instructor is doing, listen to what's being said, and try to assimilate what is being communicated - sometimes the differences will be more valuable than the similarities.

Seminars are often very crowded, so safety can be a real issue. Keep your eyes open and be aware of the people training around you. A good but often overlooked approach is to always "throw to the outside" (i.e. towards the edge of the tatami) rather than into the centre. If there are really too many people on the mat to practise safely, either just take your partner to the point of balance, or train in small group. If training in groups, try to keep them small (no more than 6 people) or you'll spend more time standing in the queue than actually practising!

As comfortable as it is to train with people you know, there is more value to practising with new people, and the differences in ability, weight, height, strength and flexibility will all add to your experience, and ultimately benefit your Aikido. A good idea is to try to practise with students of the instructor teaching the session, they will be more familiar with the methods and movements, and by "feeling" the way they practise, you should gain better understanding of what is being taught.

Don't try to remember everything that is shown! Concentrate on what the instructor is demonstrating, and try to replicate the movements shown the best you can - even if you go away having picked up only one new idea or principle, you have had a good day!

Most importantly, have a good time, on and off the mat. Most day or weekend seminars will include an evening social event, and these are a great opportunity to get to know people better.

We in Aikido are one family. In the beginning all Aikido came from the one source, that of O Sensei. Many students sat at his feet and trained but due to their varying sizes, ages, attitudes, abilities and being with O Sensei at various times of his and Aikido's development, they experienced and subsequently interpreted Aikido in many different ways, resulting in the varying styles of Aikido we have today.

In my early years of study all I wanted to do was to train with friends at my dojo and I was nervous about attending seminars. It is said by many great teachers that one should train with one teacher until Dan grade then go out and train with others to broaden one's knowledge, experience and to gain a more rounded understanding of Aikido. The attendance at courses and seminars I feel is of fundamental importance to one's study, understanding and development of Aikido, for it opens up the family of Aikido. If we were to only be in contact with our immediate parents, brothers and sisters then our knowledge of the family would be very limited. To know our cousins, aunts, uncles etc gives us a much better understanding of the family. Aikido is the same and if we want to follow and believe in the ideas and beliefs that O Sensei worked for, it is essential to attend courses and seminars with an open (beginner's) mind. I have attended many courses, seminars and visited many dojo's around the world and have been greeted with the warmth and generosity one would expect from a close family. This has given me a better understanding of Aikido in the bigger picture. We must never forget and must always be true to our original teacher, however do go and see what is out there and remember we in Aikido are one family and families should get together and support each other.

Frank Burlingham, 4th dan IA

Triangle, Circle, Square

The representation of Aikido principles by the geometrical shapes triangle, circle and square are taken from the Shinto cosmology theory of "Gogyo Gogen" where the elements of existence, Liquid, Solid and Gas are all shown to be transmutable and interrelated.

In his book "Kami no Michi", Rev. Dr. Yukitaka Yamamoto, the 96th generation Shinto High Priest (Guji) wrote:

> *"The Principle of 'Sanmi-Sangen' explains the mystery of life. Sanmi-Sangen means the three elements that constitute the basis of all forms of existence. These basic symbols both explain the meaning of and guide the destiny of human life. We can see Sanmi-Sangen operate at many levels."*

O Sensei clearly saw the relationship between this theory and the key principles of Aikido - the diagram below attempts to show how these three shapes symbolise not only the separate core principles but the inter-connectedness of all things.

The core shape of Aikido, the spiral, signified by the Circle, is apparent everywhere in the universe. The exact "5/7 logarithmic spiral", is identical in galactic discs (for example, the Milky Way), DNA strands and sub-atomic particles - O Sensei taught that Ki flows into the body in a great spiral, drawing on the power of the universe.

In simplistic terms, the Triangle represents the triangular posture predominant in Aikido, and the Square represents solidity of stance, or the principle of "weight-underside".

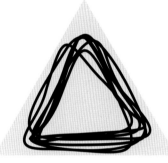

Triangle
(Iku Musubi)
Sankaku-no-Irimi
Triangular entrance
Triangular stance
Intellect
Truth
Atemi
Gas
Mission
Future
Sword
Stars
Salt
Nervous System

Circle
(Taru Musubi)
En-no-Irimi
Circular movements
Recycling of energy
Emotion
Virtue
Perfection
Liquid
Life
Present
Jewel
Moon
Water
Circulatory System

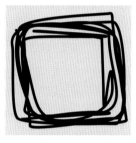

Square
(Tamatsume Musubi)
Chokusen-no-Irimi
Explosive Kokyu & Solid pinning techniques
Weight-underside
Concentration on the one point
Will
Beauty
Solid
Destiny
Past
Mirror
Sun
Rice
Digestive System

Aikido in daily life

It doesn't take a genius to see how the challenges met in Aikido mirror those in our daily lives - but it's how we respond to these challenges that is key; and in this respect the dojo becomes much more than just a place of practice, it becomes an extension of our day to day existence, reflecting upon our attitudes, reactions and health (mental, physical and spiritual).

Physical

Aikido practice promotes cardio-vascular fitness, flexibility and strength in both muscles and bones (research has shown that weight bearing and variable stress exercise such as Aikido can dramatically help reduce the onset of conditions like osteo-porosis).

With our increasingly inactive modern lifestyle, regular exercise is more important than ever. Many of us will join a gym or fitness club to build our strength and stamina, but flexibility is often neglected. Eastern medical practitioners will quote "the key to good health is a flexible spine" and, indeed, flexibility in this area not only promotes correct posture, but encourages efficient blood flow to the rest of the body (and it must be remembered that the spine protects our spinal cord, an extension of the brain and the very core of our nervous system).

Another little known benefit of stretching (present in all Aikido practice) is "neuromuscular coordination" - basically, the time it takes for an impulse to travel to the brain and back is reduced, which in turn improves the efficiency and coordination of muscle groups.

Mental / Psychological

Because our Aikido training does not refer to the body and mind as separate entities, but as part of the whole, so we find that the physical benefits of strength, flexibility and relaxation are passed over into the mental and psychological aspects of our life. Aikido training also requires the student to constantly face new challenges and learn to resolve conflict in a variety of ways. Aikido conflict-resolution techniques and ethics are increasingly being used as a tool to improve both domestic and business environments.

Spiritual

Regular practice of Aikido can teach us lessons on a cellular level - lessons we may not even realise that we are learning! Once again, the holistic approach of Aikido means that these "unlearned" lessons are available both on and off the tatami.

Detachment "indifference to outcomes" - Being too focussed on the way we want things to turn out is a great source of extreme stress.

We can bring this difficulty upon ourselves by wanting things to go too much a certain way and being inflexible in our endeavours. Releasing ourselves from being attached to the outcome of any given situation frees us from the pain and difficulty that we would otherwise cause ourselves. Acknowledging our weaknesses whilst striving for perfection is key.

Non-resistance - "to follow what is led" - Relationships on all levels benefit from an attitude of mutual acceptance - interacting with others on a symbiotic level, without attacking or maligning them. As human beings, our instinctive reaction when attacked is to react aggressively or to resist (or of course, to flee!). Aikido teaches us to go with the flow by redirecting and recycling our attacker's energy so that we are not harmed in the process, and so we find a harmonious route to a positive outcome.

Power of thoughts - "as you think so it shall be" - If we have negative thoughts about people or a generally negative attitude to life, this approach will inevitably manifest itself in our daily lives. Negative thoughts turn even good things into bad by focussing on what's wrong instead of what's right ("seeing the glass half empty" syndrome). We must constantly remind ourselves during our study of Aikido that although the techniques and exercises may be challenging, the very nature of having to overcome these challenges makes us better, stronger people

"The concept of non-resistance is one that can be easily applied to all personal interactions in both professional and private situations. It shows up in various guises such as listening to the other person, and looking for a solution instead of 'winning'.

In our Aikido training we strive to become one with our partner; 'You can't do Aikido to someone, it has to be done with them'. This extends the notion of non-resistance into blending with a situation or event to realise an outcome which could be considered "win-win". This requires an insight into both one's own and other people's motivation.

The idea of balance can be used in multiple ways. The balance of work and home life is a fairly obvious example. Maintaining your own balance can be extended from the physical not falling down, to the notion of internal integrity and truth to one's ethical framework. This covers all the compromises, large and small, that we make as we go through life.

Awareness development in Aikido as a martial art starts internally (which foot do we have forward?) and expands over time to encompass our partner (tai-jutsu), then the immediate surroundings (kokyu nage) and so on. It also can change levels from physical to mental to spiritual. Physical awareness could be that of location (I am on the mat/at home/ at work...). Mental awareness could be that of acknowledging the location (I am here to do Aikido/ play with the kids/deal with customers....) The spiritual aspect is to let your 'spirit' engage fully in the activity whatever it is so that the activity whatever it is, is exactly what you should be doing".

Ray Eder, 4th dan IA, Kyu Shin Do Aikido, NZ

Useful Japanese Words & Phrases

Ai Harmony and blending
Ai hanmi Stance where both partners have the same foot forwards
Aikido The way of universal harmony
Aikidoka Practitioner of Aikido
Aikijutsu Ancient martial art using locks and throws and co-ordination between attacker and defender
Aiki otoshi Throw also known as "the Aiki drop"
Aiki taiso The basic exercises of aikido
Ashi Leg or foot
Atemi Strike used to disturb an opponent's balance and or intent
Awase Blending or moving together
Bo Wooden staff (longer than a Jo)
Bokken Wooden sword
Bojutsu/Jojutsu The art of staff/Bo/Jo
Jo kata A set routine of exercises/movements with the Jo
Budo The Way of the Warrior
Chudan Between waist and neck
Dan Rank (of black belt)
Do The method, or "Way"
Dojo A training hall where martial arts are practised (in Zen monasteries, an area of spiritual exercises & meditation)
(Domo) Origato Gazaimasu (dommo ah-ree-gah-toe go-zah-ee-mahs) thank you (very much)
Eri Back of the collar
Gedan Below the waist
(do)Gi Martial arts training suit, normally white
Gokyo Immobilization technique similar to Ikkyo, normally practised against a tanto
Gyaku hanmi Stance where both partners have opposite feet forwards ("Gyaku" opposite)
Hakama Divided pleated skirt, worn over the Gi trousers, normally black or blue.
Hai Yes
Hanmi Stance used in Aikido with feet in "T" shape
Hanmi handachi waza Techniques performed with nage kneeling
Happo Giri/Undo Eight directional exercise ("giri" cutting, therefore practised with bokken)
Hara The centre of life energy - lower abdomen
Hasso A posture where sword or Jo held above right shoulder
Henka waza "Changing technique". To start with one technique and change into another.
Hidari Left
Hito-e-mi Triangular posture unique to Aikido

Hiji Elbow
Ikkyo First immobilisation technique
Irimi An entering movement
Irimi nage Entrance throw technique
Jiyuwasa Free style practice with random attacks from multiple attackers
Jo Wooden staff traditionally made of Japanese white oak and approx 50/51" in length
Jodan Above the neck (head/face area)
Judo The "way of suppleness/flexibility," martial style developed from jujutsu by Count Jigoro Kano, 1860-1938
Juji garami/nage Crossed/entanglement arm throw
Kaeshiwaza "Reversed/Counter Technique". Cannot be done if technique applied correctly.
Kamae A posture
Kamiza Literally means "God Seat" In Aikido, the head of the mat, usually featuring a picture of O Sensei (and/or sometimes a shrine)
Katate dori Grasped by one hand
Kaiten Circular/rotate
Kaiten nage Circular/spiral throw technique
Karate (Kara "empty", te "hand") martial art using in particular hand strikes, introduced in Japan by Funakoshi Gichin 1869-1957
Kata Formal set routine of exercises to be performed accurately and stylistically
Katana The Japanese sword
Kempo Ancient martial art related to Shaolin or Chinese boxing/Karate
Ki Life force, energy, force of the universe
Kiai "Meeting of the spirits" loud scream/cry as a physical expression of the force of Ki
Kihon Basic, fundamental
Kohai Junior student
Koshi Hips
Koshi nage Hip throw
Kote Wrist
Kote gaeshi Inner/reverse wrist turn throw (sometimes classed as an immobilisation as technique ends with a pin)
Kokyu Breath power
Kokyu dosa Breath power exercises - unbalancing your partner without using strength
Kokyu nage General term for throwing techniques - "breath throw"
Kubi Neck
Kumi tachi Advanced bokken practice in pairs
Kumi jo Advanced jo practice in pairs
Kyu Rank below shodan

Ma-ai *"Space" The appropriate distance between Uke and Nage*
Men *Face/Head*
Migi *Right*
Mune-tsuki *Blow to abdomen*
Nage *Person being "attacked" by uke and responds with movement or technique ("Thrower")*
Nagare *Flowing*
Nikkyo *2nd immobilization technique*
Obi *Belt*
Omote *Forward or to the front*
One point *The hara or centre*
O Sensei *"Great Teacher" Morihei Ueshiba, founder of Aikido*
Randori *Freestyle practice against multiple attackers (see also "juyiwaza")*
Rei *Bow*
Renzoku *Continuous*
Riai *The unified system of Body technique, bokken and Jo*
Ryote dori *Grasped with both hands*
Ryu *(Martial arts) school*
Sankyo *Third immobilisation technique*
Satori *Buddhist concept of enlightenment or the moment of total realization*
Seiza *Sitting (on the knees)*
Sempai *Senior student*
Sensei *Teacher/Instructor*
Shihan *"Teacher of teachers" a master instructor*
Shiho nage *Four direction throw (often classed as an immobilisation as this technique can finish with a pin)*
Shikko *Knee walking*
Shinai *Practice sword made from split bamboo bound with leather*
Shodan *First grade black belt*
Shomen uchi *Straight blow to the head*
Shoshin *Beginner's mind*
Soto *Outside*
Suburi *A single solo exercise using Jo or ken*
Sumi otoshi *"Corner drop" throw technique*
Suwari waza *Techniques performed on the knees*
Tachi dori *Sword taking techniques*
Taijutsu *Body techniques (performed without weapons)*
Tai no henko *"Change body to blend" basic tenkan blending practice*
Tai sabaki *Body turning*
Taiso *Exercise*
Take-musu-aiki *Abstract Aikido techniques created from a profound knowledge of the art*

Tanden *The centre of one's being*
Tanto *Knife*
Tatami *The mat on which a martial art is practised (Orig. Japanese straw floor mats)*
Tegatana *The outer edge of the hand when used as the blade of a sword*
Tenchi nage *"Heaven & Earth throw"*
Tenkan *Pivoting turn*
Tsuki *Straight thrust*
Tsugi ashi *The follow-up step*
Uchi *Strike (also can mean "inside")*
Uke *The person "attacking" nage and receiving technique*
Uchi deshi *Live-in student*
Ukemi *"Receiving through the body" (the art of escape or falling away from harm)*
Ura *To the rear or behind*
Ushiro *Behind/back/to the rear*
Yame *Stop!*
Yokomen uchi *A blow to the side of the head*
Yonkyo *Fourth immobilisation technique*
Yudansha *Holders of black belt grade*
Zanshin *Unbroken focus of attention - martial spirit which flows through all practice*
Zarei *A formal/ceremonial bow from the kneeling position*
Zori *Straw sandals worn to and from the tatami*

The History of Morihei Ueshiba, Founder of Aikido

1883 Morihei Ueshiba born December 14 in Tanabe, Kishu (Wakayama Prefecture) (father, Yoroku Ueshiba, mother, Yuki Itokawa)

1890 Goes to a Shingon sect Buddhist temple (Jizodera) to study Confucian and Buddhist scripture.

1897 Attends Tanabe Prefecture Middle School.

1899? Leaves Tanabe Prefecture Middle School and goes to Yoshida Abacus Institute.

1900? Graduates and goes to work for the Tanabe tax office as a land value assessor.

1902 Resigns from the tax office and in September moves to Tokyo to open a stationery store. Briefly studies Tenjin Shin'yo-ryu Jujutsu and Kenjutsu. Marries Hatsu Itokawa (b. 1881) a distant relative, in Tanabe.

1903 Joined 37th Army Infantry Regiment (4th Division) in Osaka.

1904 Sent to front as corporal in Russo-Japanese War. Returns as sergeant. During this time, attends Masakatsu Nakai's dojo in Sakai (Goto School of Yagyu-ryu jujutsu)

1907 Discharged from Japanese army, returns to Tanabe. Studies Kodokan judo from Kiyoichi Takagi. Awarded certificate from Goto School (Yagyu-ryu Jujutsu).

1910 Brief visit to Hokkaido. First daughter born (Matsuko).

1912 Becomes leader of the Kishu group, consisting of fifty-four households (80+ people). In March they leave Tanabe for Hokkaido. They arrive in May and settle at Shirataki, near village of Yobetsu, to start a farming community.

1915 Meets Sokaku Takeda (Daito-ryu jujitsu) at Hisada Inn in Engaru.

1917 The Shirataki community completely destroyed by fire, May 23. First son, Takemori, born in July.

1918 Elected as town councillor in Kamiyubetsu village, June 1918_April 1919.

1919 Leaves Hokkaido in December due to father's illness. Transfers land and property over to Sokaku Takeda. Meets Onisaburo Deguchi of Omoto religion in Ayabe, Kyoto Prefecture. Stays in Ayabe until December 28th.

1920 Father (Yoroku) dies on January 2, aged 76. Returns to Tanabe then relocates with his family to Ayabe (HQ of Omoto religion). Builds "Ueshiba Juku" dojo. Second son, Kuniharu born in August. Eldest son Takemori, dies in August aged 3. Second son, Kuniharu dies in September aged 1.

1921 On February 11, authorities clamp down on sect and arrest several people including Onisaburo. Third son born (Kisshomaru, but birth name Koetsu) in June.

1922 Mother, Yuki, dies. Sokaku Takeda visits Ayabe along with family to teach, staying from approx April 28 to September 15th. Awarded "Kyoji dairi" (teaching assistant) certificate from Takeda (September). Ueshiba's martial arts principles become known as Ueshiba-ryu aiki-bujutsu.

1924 Secretly leaves Ayabe on February 13th for Mongolia with Onisaburo Deguchi with concept of establishing a utopian community. The party, led by Onisaburo Deguchi, including Ueshiba, is captured and held prisoner by the Chinese military for plotting the overthrow of the government. Released after a short internment through intervention of Japanese consulate and returns to Japan. Ueshiba teaches at the Ueshiba Academy and works on the Tennodaira farm. Becomes fascinated by sojutsu (spear technique). Ueshiba reflects on his Mongolian experiences particularly facing death under gunfire. He found that he could see flashes of light indicating the path of oncoming bullets. From here on he frequently encountered situations where he felt manifestations of a spiritual force.

1925 In spring, Ueshiba is challenged by a young naval officer and master of Kendo. He defeats him without actually fighting because he could sense the direction in which the blow would fall before the officers wooden sword could strike. Immediately after this encounter, Ueshiba goes to wash at a well, and experiences "a complete serenity of body and spirit". At the same time "the unity of the universe and the self " became clear to him. It was at this time that Ueshiba changed the name of his art to Aiki-budo.

1925 Performs demonstration in Tokyo for former Prime Minister Gombei Yamamoto.

1926 In spring, Ueshiba is invited to return to Tokyo by Admiral Takeshita, where teaches at the Imperial Court and at the Imperial Household Ministry. In the summer, Ueshiba returns to Ayabe ill with an intestinal disorder.

1927 Moves to Tokyo with entire family. Establishes temporary dojo in billiard room of the Shimazu mansion in Shiba, Shirogane in Sarumachi.

1928 Moves to Shiba, Tsunamachi, site of temporary dojo.

1929 Moves with family to Shiba (near sengaku temple), Kuruma-cho, sets up temporary dojo.

1930 Moves to Shimo-Ochiai in Mejirodai. In October, Jigoro Kano of Judo observes demonstration by Ueshiba in Mejiro dojo and dispatches several students from Kodokan, including Minoru Mochizuki and Jiro Takeda, to study. Ueshiba is visited by Major General Makoto Miura, who is sceptical and only comes to defeat Ueshiba. However Miura is impressed and changes his mind. At Miura's request, Ueshiba becomes an instructor at the Toyama Military Academy.

1931 Dedication of eighty mat aiki-budo dojo inaugurated as the Kobukan dojo in Ushigome, Wakamatsu_cho. This becomes known as "hell dojo" because of the intense training.

1932 Budo Sen'yokai (Society for the Promotion of Martial Arts) is established.

1933 Ueshiba becomes president of Budo Sen'yokai. Technical manual "Budo Renshu" published. Takeda Dojo established in Hyogo Prefecture.

1935 Film documentary of Aikido Budo made in Osaka. Only known pre-war film of Morihei Ueshiba

1939 Invited to instruct in Manchuria. Fights ex sumo wrestler Tenryu and pins him with one finger.

1940 Attends martial arts demonstration in Manchuria commemorating 2600th anniversary of Japan. Aiki-budo becomes official curriculum subject at police academy. On April 30th Kobukan is granted status as an incorporated foundation by the Ministry of Health and Welfare.

1941 Aiki-budo is assimilated into the Butokukai (a government body uniting all martial arts under one organisation). Gives demonstration at Sainenkan dojo on imperial grounds for members of the imperial family. Teaches at military police academy. Invited to Manchuria to instruct during University Martial Arts week. Becomes martial arts advisor for Shimbuden and Kenkoku universities in Manchuria. The name **AIKIDO** first comes into use.

1942 Name "Aikido" becomes official and is registered with Ministry of Education. Invited to Manchuria as representative of Japanese martial arts to attend Manchuria-Japanese Exchange Martial Arts demo's in commemoration of 10th anniversary of Manchurian Independence (August). Moves to Iwama, Ibaraki Prefecture. Kisshomaru Ueshiba becomes Director of Kobukai Foundation.

1943 Aiki Shrine built in Iwama.

1945 Kobukai Foundation ceases activity due to post-war ban on martial arts. Iwama dojo completed.

1948 Hombu Dojo moves to Iwama, office opened in Tokyo. Kisshomaru Ueshiba becomes Director of Aikikai Foundation.

1949 Regular practice resumes at Tokyo dojo.

1954 Hombu Dojo moves back to Tokyo from Iwama and takes the title "Aikikai Foundation: The Hombu Dojo of Aikido".

1955 Travels to Osaka for several weeks to instruct in dojo of Bansen Tanaka.

1956 Several foreign ambassadors invited to public exhibition.

1958 U.S. television documentary "Rendezvous with Adventure" filmed

1960 Receives Medal of Honour with Purple Ribbon from Emperor Hirohito and Japanese government

1961 Invited to Hawaii by Hawaii Aikikai (February). TV documentary made by NHK company. All-Japan Student Aikido Federation established with Ueshiba as president.

1963 First All-Japan Aikido Demonstration (October).

1964 Receives Order of the Rising Sun, 4th Class, as Founder of Aikido.

1967 March 14, new Hombu Dojo building begins construction.

1968 January 12, new Hombu Dojo completed.

1969 Gives final demonstration January 15th at Kagami Biraki celebration. Dies April 26th. Ashes buried at Kozanji, Tanabe. Strands of hair preserved at Iwama, Kumano Dojo, Ayabe and Aikikai Hombu Dojo. Made honorary citizen of Tanabe and Iwama. Wife, Hatsu, dies in June.